ii

A to Z

An Everyday Devotional

ELLEN ZAKARIA ROACHELLE

Ellen Roachelle Ministries
P. O. Box 820444
North Richland Hills, Texas 76182
Elbows101@aol.com
817.471.6036

ISBN 978-0-615-66177-3

Dedication

This book is lovingly dedicated to my darling, beautiful daughter Paige.

After 30 years of pursuing me, you found me.

Between the hugs, tears and reunion, a new spunk, stamina, and

determination developed in both of our lives.

This book is for you, Paige. You have inspired me.

You have shown me that if you want something you go after it until you find

it. You are a courageous young lady.

You tenaciously searched until you found me. Giving you up at birth was the

hardest thing I've ever done. I cried many tears and you searched many years. I

thank God that the tears and years collided

and we found a missing part in both our lives.

I love you, beautiful girl, and thank God for your coming into my life.

A Note of Gratitude to a Special Lady

Nancy Harmon has generously invested into my life. This devotional would not have come to fruition if it had not been for the prodding this wonderful lady.

I met Nancy Harmon in 1967 after years of trauma. She helped me walk out of the pain into the path of righteousness. That is why I am alive today and in my right mind. I am a survivor and only look forward to a new and fulfilling life in Jesus Christ.

Traveling with her ministry, I have been given the opportunity to grace her platform, share my testimony, and help many men and women overcome their past hurts and abuses.

Nancy, an entire book could be written on the many lives you have touched through your countless hours of prayer and intercession. You never gave up on any of us. You always found good in us when we thought we had nothing good to offer.

To me, you have been a sister, a spiritual "mom," and most of all a true friend. God bless you and thank you.

Acknowledgments

First and foremost, I want to especially thank my husband Jim Roachelle. Your love and faithful support have made all the difference.

I want to express my deepest gratitude to my sister and childhood friend, Bonnie Hughes Pope. Thank you for being a faithful friend since sixth grade! Your financial support has helped bring this book into fruition.

The following people have been my faithful prayer partners, counselors, supporters, and true friends. I am sincerely thankful to God to have all of you in my life: Evangelist, singer and song writer, Nancy Harmon, Reverend Bob and Jeanette Vance, my adopted mom, B. J. Watkins, Dr. Brian and Caroline Manske, Charlie and Louelle St. Mars, Pastor Dan and Sue Helland, Tim and Lynn Cooper, Donna Hernandez, Joel and Sally Vann. Thank you, Sally, for introducing me to Nancy Harmon. Thanks to Randy Harrison, Joey and Betty Hamby, Ann Culbertson, Jackie Herman, Scott Vaughn, Dave and Pamella Vonsild, Melody Ramsey, Sharon Boland, Teresa Hurt, Carmen Swindell, Richard South, Bud Stutts, Ron, Shirley and Steven Eddy, Marilyn Dunsford, and my editor, Patricia Blais, my wonderful friend. Thank you, Miss Pat for your input and expertise.

Oh! I cannot list those who are important to me without mentioning my companion and friend, my puppy, Benny Roachelle for his unconditional love and sweet kisses!

So many faithful and wonderful friends have stood with me in much prayer. They have pushed, pulled, persuaded, and nearly dragged me into doing things I thought I could not do, but your encouragement helped me face my fears and take risks. Thank you for your love and for believing in me and making this possible.

About the Author

In 1948 I emigrated from Jerusalem to the United States with five other orphans and two adopted children and my foster parents, Richard William Schut and his wife Dorothy. The voyage from Israel to New York Harbor lasted 42 difficult days filled with chaos and confusion. What else would one expect from ten people, who were only related to each other by circumstance and not by blood, traveling across the globe to an uncertain future? Sadly, one year later, Richard died of tuberculosis and Dorothy became the lone overseer of eight children under the age of 18 in a strange land.

The loss of Richard was devastating because he was the only semblance of stability and normalcy that we had in our lives. In contrast to Richard's kind and loving nature, Dorothy was physically, sexually, emotionally, and verbally abusive. She had turned against God. She not only allowed her boyfriends to sexually abuse many of us, but she abused us, too. Her bitterness, neglect and exploitation took a terrible toll on the lives of eight innocent children. Against all odds my eldest foster brother, Al became successful with a prestigious job in the government. But Dorothy made Helaniah her slave until Helaniah married one of Dorothy's boyfriends. Alice married a good man, but came home early one day and found him in bed with Dorothy. Alice was never the same after that. Jack, Ruth and Rose were removed from the foster home because it was judged unfit and were blessed with loving, wholesome and supportive foster parents.

When I turned 18 I could not stay in the system, therefore I was alone and unprepared to face life's challenges. Life with Dorothy had been unstable and unbearable. We moved from pillar to post and the instability did little to promote confidence and security. We tried to find refuge but had no direction. We felt like the Children of Israel with Moses. Moses turned to God and found direction, but Dorothy never followed Moses' example and so she was incapable of teaching us how to depend on God's provision and wisdom. I was unsure of myself and felt ill-equipped to handle life alone.

Life with Dorothy taught me to distrust everyone. The internal conflict was debilitating. I vacillated between pining for unconditional love and acceptance and distrust which had been ingrained in me through abuse and neglect. I did not know whose arms to trust, whether they were arms offering a warm, supportive hug, or whether they were arms of exploitation.

Life started to change when Nancy Harmon came into my life. She showed me the real path to God and showed me the right way to live. I am still learning how to love and trust and receive a sense of belonging. After all these years, I am still learning how to receive hugs. This simple act of reciprocation in a loving, trusting relationship is a major accomplishment.

Nancy gave me the opportunity to grow up and live the abundant life Jesus offers. She helped me see the good in myself and brought out the good that was stuffed way down inside my walls of fear. She gave me the platform to share my testimony and song with thousands of people through hundreds of churches and television. This opportunity became valuable training. It taught me how to help others who have had similar experiences.

My sweet, tender and understanding husband offered that same unconditional love which helped me overcome my fear of trusting others. Living with me has not been easy, but his patience created an environment where I could grow and learn to trust and reciprocate love in healthy ways.

When Jesus came into my life, God became a father to this orphan girl. He picked me up out of a horrible pit and set my feet upon a rock. He established my going and my coming and gave me a new song in my mouth (See Psalm 40:2-3).

Preface

Often, when traveling with Nancy Harmon, we would be thinking about someone who had once been involved in the ministry with us, but we could not remember that person's name. One day, Nancy said, "Think, Ellen! Let's pull our thoughts together and it will eventually come to us." We would rack our brains for miles. That is when I would draw on an old habit of mine, which was to go down the alphabet from A-Z. It worked every time. The name surfaced and we'd wonder why we didn't try this trick from the very beginning.

Not too long after one particular successful brainstorming session, we wanted to find a young lady from North Carolina named Christy. She was a pastor's daughter who used to travel with Nancy Harmon Ministries. For the life of us, we could not think of the town in which she lived. We looked on the map. We made phone calls. We stretched our brains trying to remember where she lived. Finally, after all that fruitless effort had been expended, Nancy said, "Ellen, go down the alphabet. Maybe something will ring a bell." Bells rang about an hour later as I went from A to Z and searched the towns on the map. Troy, North Carolina! Hallelujah! The alphabet did not let us down.

This habit of using the alphabet to bring important information to mind is the inspiration for this devotional. Let it be a reminder of who God is in you and who you are in Him. Add some goodies and thoughts of your own. It works for all ages and you can enjoy this more than a onetime read.

A

God is my *Alpha*, my *advocate*, the *Almighty* and my *All-Sufficient One*. I have *abundant* life in Him. I can *abide* in Him and He *abides* in me. He is *always* with me, and He promised to never leave me. He is *all-together* lovely. He is my *answer* to every question and every dilemma. He *adopted* me and *accepted* me, just as I was, without one plea.

The opposite of who He is to me is *adversity, anger, animosity, abnormal* and *aloneness*. I embrace Him today and let these things go. My prayer is, "Lord, let me be an instrument of your love and abundance. Let the abundance that flows from my innermost being be a blessing and not cursing into someone else's life. Out of the abundance of my mouth, let me speak good and not evil. It is my choice."

Scriptures

Revelation 1:8, 11	John 15:1-11
1 John 2:1	Matthew 28:20
Genesis 17:1	Song of Solomon 5:16
Genesis 22:14	Romans 8:15
John 10:10	Ephesians 1:6
Matthew 12:35	

If you know it, sing this song now and several times throughout your day to remind you of who you are *in Christ,* who He is and what He can do *in you*, and what you can do *in Him*.

Amazing Grace

Amazing grace! how sweet the sound,
That saved a wretch like me!
I once was lost, but now am found,
Was blind, but now I see.

The Lord has promised good to me,
His word my hope secures;
He will my shield and portion be
As long as life endures.

Written by:
Niente A.
Lyrics: Sony/Atv Music
Publishing Company. LLC, Curb Music

Answer these questions: 1. Which statement stands out to me the most? 2. How could my life be different if I truly believed it were true? 3. What am I willing to change today to move forward?

_____

_____

_____

_____

_____

_____

_____

Proverbs 3:5-6

Trust in the LORD with all your heart,
And lean not on your own understanding;
In all your ways acknowledge Him,
And He shall direct your paths.

ASSURANCE

These things I have written to you who believe
in the name of the Son of God,
that you may know that you have eternal life,
and that you may continue
to believe in the name of the Son of God
(1 John 5:13).

B

God is the *breath* that I *breathe*. He is my *brother*, *branch*, and *bread* when I am hungry. I will *bless* the Lord at all times. His praise shall continually be in my mouth. I will *boast* of Him at all times. He shed His innocent *blood* for my salvation. *Behold* the Lamb of God who took away the sins of the world.

He is the *Balm in Gilead* that mends, heals and soothes. He is the Lord of the *breakthrough* who breaks all the barriers which try to hold me back. I will not *bend* or *bow* to anything this world has to offer. I will *build* myself up in my most holy faith. I will *build* others up. I will *bless* those who curse me and say all manner of evil against me. I will *bless* the Lord at all times and will not forget all His *benefits*.

Life is not easy. I have a choice to become *bitter*—harsh, tart, resentful and cynical. Or, I can choose to become *better*—enhanced, improved, developed and advanced. No matter what happens, I am not a victim but a victor.

Scriptures

Genesis 2:7	Jeremiah 8:22
Romans 8:29	1 Chronicles 14:11
Isaiah 11:1	Daniel 3:15-18
John 6:51	Jude 1:20
Psalm 34:2, 44:8	Matthew 5:44
Ephesians 1:4, 7	Psalm 103:2

If you know them, sing these songs now and several times throughout your day to remind you of who you are *in Christ,* who He is and what He can do *in you,* and what you can do *in Him.*

There is a Fountain Filled With Blood

There is a fountain filled with blood,
Drawn from Emmanuel's veins.
And sinners can plunge beneath that flood,
And lose all their guilty stains.
Lose all their guilty stains, lose all their guilty stains.
And sinners plunge beneath that flood,
Wash all their sins away.

Written by: William Cowper (1731-1800)

The Blood Will Never Lose Its Power.

The blood that Jesus shed for me,
Way back on dark Calvary,
It's that blood that gives me strength,
From day to day,
It will never lose its power.

For it reaches to the highest mountain
And it flows to the lowest valley,
It's that blood that gives me strength from day to day,
It will never lose its power.

Andre Crouch (BMI)

Answer these questions: 1. Which statement stands out to me the most? 2. How could my life be different if I truly believed it were true? 3. What am I willing to change today to move forward?

_____

_____

_____

_____

_____

_____

_____

Mark 9:23

Jesus said to him, "If you can believe,
all things are possible to him who believes."

Blessing and not cursing

"You have heard that it was said,
'You shall love your neighbor
and hate your enemy. But I say to you,
love your enemies, bless those who curse you,
do good to those who hate you,
and pray for those who spitefully use you
and persecute you
(Matthew 5:43-44).

C

Jesus is my *cornerstone*. He is the *center* of my joy. I can *cast* my *cares* on Him. He will *carry* the weight of the world on His shoulders, so that means He will *carry* my burdens. He *causes* me to triumph. *Christ* in me is my hope of glory. He *clothes* me with honor and majesty. I am more than a *conqueror* through Him who loves me. I have *confidence* knowing that He will see me through. He will *calm* my fears. He *calls* me his own. He makes me *clean*.

He makes me *capable,* giving me sufficient power to put every enemy under my feet. The *chains* of sin are broken off of my life. I am part of a *chosen generation*. I am *cherished* and treated with tenderness. I am a *citizen* of the household of faith. I can have sweet *communion* with Him. I am a *carrier* of the cross of Christ.

I am *committed* and dedicated to Him. He is my "sane asylum," my haven, my shelter, my sanctuary and my protection. He teaches me sensible and sound doctrine, which keeps me sane. He is my *Creator*.

Scriptures

Isaiah 28:16	Psalm 34:4
John 15:11	1 John 1:9
1 Peter 5:7	Mark 6:3
Matthew 11:28	2 Corinthians 4:7
2 Corinthians 2:14	2 Peter 2:4
Colossians 1:27	1 Peter 2:9
Psalm 21:5	Galatians 6:10
Romans 8:37	Romans 12:1-2
Hebrews 1:16	

If you know it, sing this song now and several times throughout your day to remind you of who you are *in Christ,* who He is and what He can do *in you,* and what you can do *in Him.*

Conqueror

I am a conqueror,
I am made whole,
I am a conqueror,
Body, mind, and soul

I am a conqueror,
I am His own,
I am a conqueror,
And I belong.

Written by: Nancy Harmon (BMI)
Written for: Ellen Roachelle

Answer these questions: 1. Which statement stands out to me the most? 2. How could my life be different if I truly believed it were true? 3. What am I willing to change today to move forward?

_____

_____

_____

_____

_____

_____

_____

1 Peter 5:6-7

Therefore humble yourselves under the mighty hand of God, that He may exalt you in due time, casting all your care upon Him, for He cares for you.

JESUS IS THE CORNERSTONE

Therefore thus says the Lord God,
Behold I am laying in Zion
for a foundation a Stone,
a tested Stone, a precious Cornerstone
of sure foundation;
he who believes (trusts in, relies on,
and adheres to that Stone)
will not be ashamed or give way
or hasten away [in sudden panic]
(Isaiah 28:16, *Amplified Bible*).

D

J esus *died* for me. He is my *deliverer* and my *defense*. He is my *Daystar* and my *Dayspring*. When I *delight* in Him, He will give me the *desires* of my heart. He is my *destiny*. He is my *doctor*. He turned my *darkness* into light. He erased my *debts*. He *delights* in me He opens *doors* that no man can shut and shuts *doors* that no man can open. He sweat *drops* of blood for me. When I *draw* close to Him, He *draws* close to me. He *died* to give me abundant life.

I am *devoted* and *dedicated* to Him. I am *desperate* for Him. I am a born-again, *delivered disciple*. I am a learner. I can *depend*, rest and rely solely in and on Him. I hold my head up high with *dignity* as I *draw* closer to Him. In my *distress*, I call on Him. In my anger I cry unto Him. In my affliction, I call unto Him and He will never turn a *deaf* ear to me. *Daily* I will *draw* from the wells of living waters of salvation. I want to be not only a hearer but a *doer* of the Word. I am *devoted* to my *deliverer*, Jesus Christ. I am *determined*, even if it takes *dying* for Him. I *dare* to be like *Daniel*. I can *do* all things through Christ who strengthens me. I have *dignity* appropriated by His loving kindness and grace. I am *depending* on Jesus to see me through. I *desire* to *do* the will of my Father. I *delight* in Him.

Scriptures

Romans 5:8
Romans 11:26
2 Peter 1:19
Luke 1:78
Psalm 37:4
Romans 8:29
Luke 5:31

Psalm 139:7-8
Luke 22:44
Hebrews 10:22
John 10:10
Psalm 118:5
Isaiah 59:1
James 1:25

Scriptures (Continued)

Colossians 1:13   Philippians 4:13
Colossians 2:14

If you know it, sing this song now and several times throughout your day to remind you of who you are *in Christ,* who He is and what He can do *in you,* and what you can do *in Him.*

Down at the Cross (AKA Glory to His Name)

Down at the cross where my savior died,
Down where for cleansing from sin I cried.
There to my heart was the blood applied.
Glory to His name.

I am so wondrously saved from sin.
Jesus so sweetly abides within.
There at the cross where He took me in.
Glory to His name

Written by: Elisha A. Huffman (1878)

Answer these questions: 1. Which statement stands out to me the most? 2. How could my life be different if I truly believed it were true? 3. What am I willing to change today to move forward?

_____

_____

_____

_____

_____

_____

_____

Psalm 37:4

Delight yourself also in the LORD,
And He shall give you the desires of your heart.

16

DELIGHT YOURSELF IN THE LORD

Dwell in the land,
and feed on His faithfulness.
Delight yourself also in the Lord,
and He shall give you the desires
of your heart
(Psalm 37:3b-4).

E

Jesus is *Eternal Life*. He is my *Everlasting Father*. He is the *elect of God*. He is my true *example*. He is my *encourager*. He *embraces* me; He *edifies* me, and lifts me up and allows me to sit in heavenly places. He is *enduring*. He is my *escape* from temptation and from hell. He has *established* me. He has *esteemed* me.

He is *excellent* in all his ways. He lends His *ear* to me; He has the distinguishing power to regard my plea. He *edies* me and improves me. He makes me *eligible* and worthy to be chosen. He *empowers* me. He *enlarges* my borders to set me free. He *enlightens* me and makes my way clear. He sets my feet upon a rock and *establishes* me to make me stable.

I was in a horrible pit, but Jesus stooped down and picked me up, set me upon a rock and gave me a new song to sing for Him. He has *enveloped* me in His arms of love. He has covered me with His feathers. Underneath me are His *everlasting* arms. I am *established* in Him.

I will *earnestly* seek Him, both day and night. My *ears* will be in tune with His heart and His still small voice. I will hold up my head with *elegance* and *excellence* because of His *embellishments*. He *establishes* me and He is from *everlasting* to *everlasting*.

Scriptures

1 John 5:12	Psalm 40:2
Isaiah 9:6	Isaiah 36:7
Colossians 3:12	Isaiah 54:2
Ephesians 5:1	Psalm 91:4
Psalm 19:9	Psalm 103:17

If you know it, sing this song now and several times throughout your day to remind you of who you are *in Christ,* who He is and what He can do *in you,* and what you can do *in Him.*

Everybody Ought to Know

Everybody ought to know,
Everybody ought to know,
Everybody ought to know,
Who Jesus is.

He's the Lily of the valley,
He's the bright and morning star,
He's the fairest of ten thousand,
Everybody ought to know.

Public Domain: Written for children

Answer these questions: 1. Which statement stands out to me the most? 2. How could my life be different if I truly believed it were true? 3. What am I willing to change today to move forward?

_____

_____

_____

_____

_____

_____

_____

John 5:24

Most assuredly, I say to you, he who hears My word and believes in Him who sent Me has everlasting life, and shall not come into judgment, but has passed from death into life.

ESTABLISHED IN THE FAITH

*As you have therefore
received Christ Jesus the Lord,
so walk in Him
rooted and built up in Him
and established in the faith...*
(Colossians 2:6b-7a).

F

Jesus is *faithful*. He is my *Father* and my *friend*. He never *fails* or *forsakes* me. He wants to have *fellowship* with me daily. He is the author and *finisher* of my *faith*. He is the *first*. He has *freed* me from the curse of the law. He has *forgiven* me. He is the one who *found* me when I was lost. He is my *fountain* and my *foundation*. He is the *fairest* of ten thousand.

I have *faith* and confidence in Him. I can *fight* the good *fight of faith*. I have no guilt for my past because He has *forgiven* me. I have *favor* with Him. He has become my *Father*, one who has no ill intensions toward me. I am His adopted child and He holds me close during the storms of life.

When *fear* comes knocking at my door, He says, "*Fear* not, My child, for I am with you. I will never leave you, nor *forsake* you." Because He *fought* for my freedom, I have no need to *fight* for my rights in Him. He is a mighty *fortress* that I can run into and hide, knowing that He is my *forever friend* and *Father*.

There is no *fear* in love, for perfect love casts out all *fear*. At least 365 times, the Bible tells me "*Fear* not." That is at least one time for every day! I have no need to *fear* because He loves me.

If all I have is mustard-seed-sized *faith*, I have *faith* enough to move mountains!

Scriptures

Deuteronomy 7:9   1 John 1:9
Romans 8:15   Revelation 21:6
John 15:14   1 Corinthians 3:11
Hebrews 13:5   Hebrews 1:16

Scriptures (Continued)

1 Corinthians 1:9	1 Timothy 6:12
Hebrews 12:2	Ephesians 1:5
Revelation 1:11	1 John 4:18
Galatians 3:13	Luke 17:6

If you know it, sing this song now and several times throughout your day to remind you of who you are *in Christ,* who He is and what He can do *in you*, and what you can do *in Him*.

Great is Thy Faithfulness

Great is thy faithfulness,
Oh, God my father.
There is no shadow of turning with thee.
Thou changest not.
Your compassions, they fail not.
As thou hast been, thou forever will be.

Great is thy faithfulness,
Great is thy faithfulness.
Morning by morning new mercies I see.

All I have needed,
Your hand has provided,
Great is thy faithfulness,
Lord unto me.

(Public Domain: Written by: Thomas Chisolm)

Answer these questions: 1. Which statement stands out to me the most? 2. How could my life be different if I truly believed it were true? 3. What am I willing to change today to move forward?

_____

_____

_____

_____

_____

_____

_____

1 John 1:9

If we confess our sins, He is faithful and just to forgive us our sins and to cleanse us from all unrighteousness.

HIS FAITHFULNESS

*Let us hold fast the confesssion
of our hope without wavering,
for He who promised is faithful*
(Hebrews 10:23).

G

Jesus is my *Great God Jehovah*. He is my *Good Shepherd*. He is the *glory* and the lifter of my head. He is the *gift* of life. He is my *gardener* who continually pulls the weeds out of my life. He is full of *good* works. He is *guiltless*. He is my *guide*. He is *gracious* to perform. He is full of *grace* and truth.

I have a *God* who is *gracious* and His wonders to perform. When He looks at me, I believe He says, "I have created something *good*." I am whole, useful, valuable, virtuous, adequate, valid and able. His *grace* is sufficient for me. He *grafted* me into the vine to support me and *give* me the nourishment necessary to sustain me and cause me to flourish and bear good fruit that endures the test of time.

I will *glorify* and honor Him forever. He is my *Good Shepherd* who leads me beside still waters. He restores my soul. He leads me through paths of righteousness. Though I may walk through the valley of the shadow of death, He is with me. His rod and staff comfort me.

His *grace* pardons me and cleanses me from all unrighteousness. His *grace* is *greater* than all of my sins.

Scriptures

Genesis 22:13
John 10:11, 14
Psalm 3:3
1 John 5:12
John 15:1
John 10:32
Hebrews 4:15

John 14:26
Joel 2:13
2 Corinthians 12:9
John 15:5
John 15:16
1 John 1:9

If you know it, sing this song now and several times throughout your day to remind you of who you are *in Christ,* who He is and what He can do *in you,* and what you can do *in Him.*

My Tribute (To God be the Glory)

How can I say thanks
For the things He has done for me?
Things so undeserved,
Yet He gave to prove His love for me.

The voices of a million angels
Could not express my gratitude
All that I am or ever hope to be,
I owe it all to Him.

To God be the Glory,
To God be the Glory,
To God be the Glory
For the things He has done.
With His blood He saved me.
With His power He raised me,
To God be the Glory
For the things He has done.

Andre Crouch

Answer these questions: 1. Which statement stands out to me the most? 2. How could my life be different if I truly believed it were true? 3. What am I willing to change today to move forward?

_____

_____

_____

_____

_____

_____

_____

Psalm 104:1

Bless the LORD, O my soul! O LORD my God, You are very great;
You are clothed with honor and majesty.

GUIDANCE

*If any of you lacks wisdom,
let him ask of God,
who gives to all liberally
and without reproach,
and it will be given to him
(James 1:5).*

H

Jesus is my *healer*, the *head* of my life, the *hands* that gently lead and guide me, like those of a skilled potter with clay. He is my *helper*. His *heart* is turned toward me. He is my *heavenly Father*. He is my *high priest*. He is *holy*, *honest*, and He is my *hope*. He is *honorable*. He is *hospitable*, always making room for one more and keeping the house clean and presentable. He is *humble* and meek of heart.

I have a sound mind because of Him. I have freedom from disease. He has opened up His *heart* which is the seat of His affections. He is my *Helper*, always giving me the strength toward affecting a purpose for me. He *holds* me with a grasp that will never let go. He supports me while *holding* me with His truth. He holds me in *holiness*, a state of quality with *high morals*. He keeps me *holy* and free from sin. He keeps me *honest* and upright. I *honor* Him. He gives me *hope* so that I can desire good, attainable things. When I do not know what tomorrow may bring, He *holds* my hand and says that it will be all right in the morning. Without my *hope* in Jesus, I would be *horribly* miserable! Has not the potter power over the clay?

Scriptures

Exodus 15:26	1 Peter 1:16
Ephesians 5:23	Romans 12:13
Isaiah 64:8	Matthew 11:29
John 14:26	Hebrews 1:3
Matthew 6:26	1 John 3:3
Hebrews 4:14	

If you know it, sing this song now and several times throughout your day to remind you of who you are *in Christ,* who He is and what He can do *in you,* and what you can do *in Him.*

He Hideth My Soul

A wonderful Savior is Jesus my Lord,
A wonderful Savior to me,
He hideth my soul in the cleft of the rock,
Where rivers of pleasure I see.

He hideth my soul in the cleft o the rock,
That shadows a dry thirsty land,
He hideth my life in the depths of His love,
And covers me there with His hand.

By Frances J. Crosby

Answer these questions: 1. Which statement stands out to me the most? 2. How could my life be different if I truly believed it were true? 3. What am I willing to change today to move forward?

_____

_____

_____

_____

_____

_____

_____

Psalm 51:10-11

Create in me a clean heart, O God,
And renew a steadfast spirit within me. Do not cast me away from Your
presence, And do not take Your Holy Spirit from me.

HANDLING PRESSURE

God is our refuge and strength
A very present help in trouble.
Therefore we will not fear
(Psalm 46:1-2a).

I

Jesus is my *Idol*. He is my *Instructor*. He is my *Intercessor*. He is my *Inspiration*. He is *integrity*. He is the *investor* in my life who handles all of my personal *investments*. He *inclines* His ears to me and listens to the cry of my heart. He wants *intimacy* with me. He *included* me when He passed out His blessings because He is no respecter of persons.

Jesus is the One I *idolize*. I worship Him and adore Him alone. I set my affections on Him. I submerge myself in Him. When I "plunge into Him," I can rest *in Him,* safe from outward pressures because my life is hid with God *in Christ*. I want more of Him and less of me. I am complete *in Him*.

He has *inclined* His ear to me to hear my words, desires, needs, and wants. He wants to *increase* my life by making things greater and advanced in quality. He wants me to profit as my soul prospers. He wants me to *indulge* myself with His favor. He spoils me with good and extra special gifts because I am His child.

When I try to do the *impossible*, it becomes *impossibility*, because of the "*I*." The *impossible* can only be done through Christ…*I can* do all things through Jesus Christ who strengthens me. All things are possible with God.

Scriptures

Exodus 20:3
John 14:26
Hebrews 7:25
Ephesians 1:17-18
1 Corinthians 1:9
Acts 10:34

Acts 10:34
Colossians 3:3
Colossians 2:10
Psalm 116:2
2 Corinthians 9:10
Philippians 4:13

If you know it, sing this song now and several times throughout your day to remind you of who you are *in Christ,* who He is and what He can do *in you,* and what you can do *in Him.*

Draw Me Nearer (I am Thine Oh, Lord)

I am thine, oh, Lord,
I have heard your voice,
And it told thy love to me.
But I long to rise,
In the arms of faith,
And be closer drawn to thee.

Draw me nearer, nearer, blessed Lord,
To the cross where thou hast died,
Draw me nearer, nearer, blessed Lord,
To thy precious bleeding side.

By: Frances J. Crosby

Answer these questions: 1. Which statement stands out to me the most? 2. How could my life be different if I truly believed it were true? 3. What am I willing to change today to move forward?

_____

_____

_____

_____

_____

_____

_____

Psalm 16:5-6

You, O LORD, are the portion of my inheritance and my cup; You maintain my lot. The lines have fallen to me in pleasant places; Yes, I have a good inheritance.

IMITATION

But imitate those who
through faith and patience
inherit the promises
(Hebrews 6:12b).

J

Jesus is my *Judge*, my *jury*, my *joy*. He *justified* me. He is the Great God *Jehovah*. He is *jealous* over me. I am a *joint-heir* with Him.

He is my Savior, my salvation. As my *Judge*, He is my discerner, the one who can distinguish and know the difference and detects all things. He is my moderator, my authority, my critic. He is *just*, fair-minded and impartial.

I am *justified*, acquitted and declared righteous through His blood. I am now in right-standing with Him who sits on the throne. The *joy* of the Lord is my strength. I delight to do His will.

Scriptures

Acts 10:42
John 15:11
Psalm 83:18
Exodus 34:14

Isaiah 45:21
Romans 5:1
Nehemiah 8:12

If you know them, sing these songs now and several times throughout your day to remind you of who you are *in Christ,* who He is and what He can do *in you,* and what you can do *in Him.*

Jesus, Lord to Me

Jesus, Jesus Lord to me,
Master, Savior, Prince of Peace,
Ruler of my heart to thee,
Jesus Lord to me...

(Chorus) By: Yellow House

Prayerfully sing this song, by Janet Paschal.

When I speak the Name of Jesus,
Oh the peace that fills my soul;
Tenderly He tries to woo me,
Back into the narrow way,
Jesus, oh how sweet the melody,
Earth had known no sweeter frame,
Precious Lord, precious redeemer,
Jesus, Jesus is His name...

Written by: Janet Paschal,
Performed by: Nancy Harmon/BMI

Answer these questions: 1. Which statement stands out to me the most? 2. How could my life be different if I truly believed it were true? 3. What am I willing to change today to move forward?

_____

_____

_____

_____

_____

_____

_____

Psalm 16:11

You will show me the path of life; In Your presence is fullness of joy; At Your right hand are pleasures forevermore.

JOY

I have no greater joy
than to hear that my children
walk in truth
(3 John 4).

K

Jesus is my *Keeper*. He is *kind*. He is the *King* of all kings. He *knows* all things. He *knits* me together the way He designed me to be. He calls me a *King's kid*.

Jesus will *keep* me in peace as my mind is fixed on Him. He preserves me and holds me. He is *kind* to me, showing me compassion, gentleness, benevolence, thoughtfulness and consideration.

I am safe with Him because He is tender toward me. I can trust Him with my most intimate thoughts, hopes, and dreams. I do not have to fear because of His loving kindness toward me.

Scriptures

Galatians 3:29
Lamentations 3:22-23
Revelation 19:16
John 14:26

John 18:4
Isaiah 26:3
1 John 4:18

If you know it, sing this song now and several times throughout your day to remind you of who you are *in Christ*, who He is and what He can do *in you*, and what you can do *in Him*.

42

King's Kid

Chorus

Just call me a King's kid,
I know just who I am,
I'm a Holy child,
I'm the seed of Abraham,
A righteous one,
'Been redeemed by the blood of the Lamb
And the only King of Kings is 'kin to me.

Song by Nancy Harmon/BMI

Answer these questions: 1. Which statement stands out to me the most? 2. How could my life be different if I truly believed it were true? 3. What am I willing to change today to move forward?

_____

_____

_____

_____

_____

_____

_____

John 14:23

"If anyone loves Me, he will keep My word; and my Father will love him, and We will come to him and make Our home with him.

KINDNESS

And be kind to one another,
tenderhearted, forgiving one another,
just as God in Christ also forgave you
(Ephesians 4:32).

L

Jesus is the *Lion* of Judah. He is the *Lamb* of God, the *Light* of the world. He is *Living* bread. He is the *Lord* of lords. He is *Love*. He is the *Lily* of the valley. He is the *Law* and my *liberty*. He is *Life*. There is no *limit* to His *Love* and grace. He is *long-suffering*. He is the *Lord* of hosts. He is the *love* of God. His *love* is unconditional. He is *lovely*. He was made *lower* than the angels to give me *life* and *liberty*. Jesus and I *labor* together. He is the *lover* of my soul. He is my commander and chief. He gives me *liberty* and has made me free.

I am *led* by the Spirit of God. He is the *Lord* of my life. He is my ruler, my *light*. I can see in the darkness because He is the *lamp* unto my feet and the *light* of the world. I follow His *law*, rules, and statutes. I know the way to go because He shows me. Because of Him, I have *life* and *life* more abundantly. In Him I live and move and have my being. I am a *lump* of clay in the palm of His hands.

Scriptures

Revelation 5:5	2 Corinthians 3:17
John 1:29	2 Corinthians 6:1
John 8:12	1 Timothy 1:16
John 6:51	Psalm 119:105
Revelation 17:14	John 10:10
1 John 4:16	Isaiah 64:8
Song of Solomon 2:1	

If you know it, sing this song now and several times throughout your day to remind you of who you are *in Christ,* who He is and what He can do *in you*, and what you can do *in Him*.

Leaning on the Everlasting Arms

What a fellowship,
What a joy divine,
Leaning on the everlasting arms,
What a blessedness,
What a peace is mine,
Leaning on the everlasting arms.

Leaning, leaning safe and secure from all alarm,
Leaning, leaning, leaning on the everlasting arms.

By: Anthony J. Showalter and Elisha a. Hoffman

Answer these questions: 1. Which statement stands out to me the most? 2. How could my life be different if I truly believed it were true? 3. What am I willing to change today to move forward?

_____

_____

_____

_____

_____

_____

_____

Revelation 5:11-12

Then I looked, and I heard…thousands of thousands saying with a loud voice; "Worthy is the Lamb who was slain To receive power and riches and wisdom, And strength and honor and glory and blessing!"

48

GOD'S KIND OF LOVE

Love...bears all things,
believes all things,
hopes all things,
endures all things
(See 1 Corintians 13:4-8).

M

Master of the wind, Jesus is the One who quiets my storms. He is my *Messiah*, the *Mighty* God. He is my m*ediator*, my m*anna* and my m*entor*. He is my *Maker*.

He is the *Man* of sorrows, so He is always *merciful* to me. He is *meek* and humble of heart. He performs *miracles* and *moves mountains*. He is *marvelous*. He is my *melody*. He is a *multiplier*. He is my bright and *Morning Star*.

He is my *mender*, the one who restores my life and makes me brand new. I have a better state of mind than I had before He came into my life.

Because He did not spare His own life, I am forgiven, I am constantly in His thoughts, on His *mind* and in His prayers. I can follow the example He sets. I can have His *mind*, one with sound thoughts and sound judgment and understanding. I can sing a new song and my joy is restored.

Scriptures

Mark 4:41	Matthew 11:29
John 1:29	John 3:2
Isaiah 9:6	Mark 11:23
1 Timothy 2:5	Revelation 22:16
John 6:58	2 Corinthians 5:17
Job 36:3	1 Corinthians 2:16
Isaiah 53:3	Hebrews 7:25
Luke 6:36	

If you know it, sing this song now and several times throughout your day to remind you of who you are *in Christ,* who He is and what He can do *in you*, and what you can do *in Him.*

Master of the Wind

I know the Master of wind,
I know the maker of the rain,
He can calm the storm,
Cause the sun to shine again,
I know the Master of the wind.

By: Joel and LaBreeska Hemphill

Answer these questions: 1. Which statement stands out to me the most? 2. How could my life be different if I truly believed it were true? 3. What am I willing to change today to move forward?

_____

_____

_____

_____

_____

_____

_____

Psalm 93:4

The LORD on high is mightier Than the noise of many waters, Than the mighty waves of the sea.

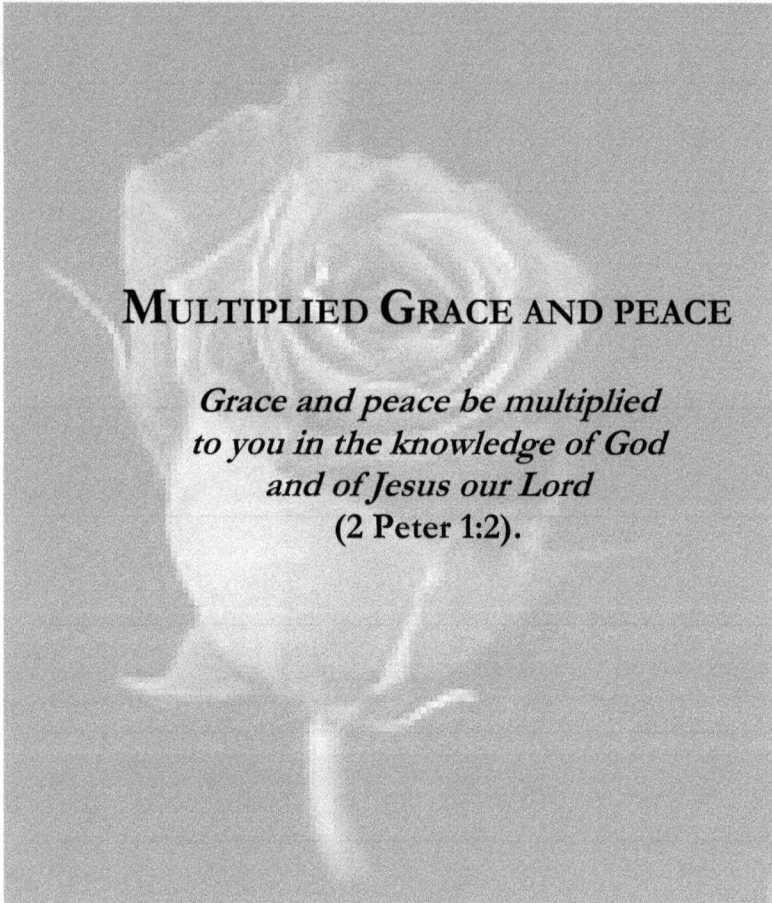

MULTIPLIED GRACE AND PEACE

*Grace and peace be multiplied
to you in the knowledge of God
and of Jesus our Lord
(2 Peter 1:2).*

N

Jesus is the *Name* above all names. He is always *near*. He is *noble*. He *Never* lies; what He says is dependable. He will *never* leave me or forsake me. He is my *nourishment*. He is the *Nazarene*.

I can call on His *name* in any circumstance and His power and influence will lift me above my circumstances. Because He is dependable, I am who He says I am and I can do what He says I can do. I am fed with His Word and in doing His will. I sing a *new* song because *nothing* is impossible with Him. When I draw *nigh* unto Him, He draws *nigh* unto me and I feel Him *near* me all of the time. I am *never* alone because He is always with me. He is as close to me as the mention of His *Name*.

Scriptures

Philippians 2:9	Matthew 2:23
John 14:18	Romans 10:13
Numbers 23:19	Psalm 144:9
Hebrews 13:5	Luke 1:37
John 6:35	

If you know it, sing this song now and several times throughout your day to remind you of who you are *in Christ,* who He is and what He can do *in you*, and what you can do *in Him*.

Nothing's Too Big For God

Nothing's too big for my God, no, no, no, no,
Nothing's too big for my God.
'Not going to be discouraged,
'Not going to be depressed,
Nothing's too big for God and I'm in His rest.

By: Nancy Harmon/BMI

Answer these questions: 1. Which statement stands out to me the most? 2. How could my life be different if I truly believed it were true? 3. What am I willing to change today to move forward?

_____

_____

_____

_____

_____

_____

_____

Psalm 72:19

And blessed be His glorious name forever! And let the whole earth be filled with His glory. Amen and Amen.

His Name

*"For where two or more
are gathered together in My name,
I am there in the midst of them"*
(Matthew 18:20).

O

Jesus is *Ointment* being poured forth. He is an *Over-comer*. He is *omnipresent*, *omnipotent* and *omniscient*. He daily *opens* the windows of heaven and pours out blessings too large to contain. He is the *only* wise God.

He was *obedient*, even to going to the cross.

As His *ointment* pours over me, I am healed and restored by the anointing that destroys the yokes of bondage in my life.

I want to *obey* Him, because He works within me, both to will and to do of His good pleasure. I want to be submissive to His authority and to comply with His commands and requirements. I want to be *objective* and belong to His cause and give my loyalty to it. I want to *observe* and take notice and behold His attention. I want to celebrate Him. I want to *obtain*, possess, acquire and hold good His possessions which He has freely given me. I want to be an *oracle*, wise and authoritative in utterance. I want to be in His *order* and be established with dignity. I want to *overflow*, spread *over*, and to be so full of Jesus that His contents run over and about with superabundance.

I am an *overcomer* through Him. Life and the devil do not overcome me. I overcome them through His power working in and through me.

Scriptures

Jeremiah 8:22	Malachi 3:10
Revelation 12:11	1 Timothy 1:17
Matthew 28:20	Philippians 2:8
Micah 3:8	Philippians 2:13
1 John 3:20	1 John 4:4

If you know it, sing this song now and several times throughout your day to remind you of who you are *in Christ,* who He is and what He can do *in you,* and what you can do *in Him.*

O Happy Day

O happy day,
That fixed my soul,
On thee my savior and my God!
Well, may this glowing heart rejoice,
And tell its raptures all abroad.

Out of bondage, sorrow and night,
Jesus I come, Jesus I come;
Into the freedom,
Gladness and light,
Jesus I come, Jesus I come.
Out of our shame,
Failure, loss, fear and dread,
And arrogant pride, Jesus I come to thee.

By: Roland Schneider

Answer these questions: 1. Which statement stands out to me the most? 2. How could my life be different if I truly believed it were true? 3. What am I willing to change today to move forward?

_____

_____

_____

_____

_____

_____

_____

Psalm 130:1

Out of the depths I have cried to You, O Lord; Lord, hear my voice!
Let Your ears be attentive To the voice of my supplications.

OVERCOMING FAITH

*"These things I have spoken to you,
that in Me you may have peace.
In the world you will have tribulation;
but be of good cheer,
I have overcome the world"*
(John 16:33).

P

God has *pardoned* me by placing my sin and guilt on Jesus, who took pain for my *pardon*. He gave me a new *path* to walk. He *pursued* and *persuaded* me. He is *patient* with me. He is the *peace* that passes all understanding. He is *perfection*. He is the *pearl* of great *price*. He is a *pillar* that I can lean on. He is my *physician*. He is the God of *plenty*. He is my *prophet* and *pastor*. It is His *pleasure* to give me His kingdom. He is *powerful*. All things are *possible* through Him. He is my *potentate*. He is Jehovah Jireh, the Lord my *provider*; He is more than enough of what I need.

As His child, I can be a *partaker* with Him. I want to be not only a *partaker*, but a *participant*, and a *partner* with Him. Through my trust in Him, I can experience the *peace* of God which passes all understanding. I can share my faith with others while I have unbroken fellowship with Jesus. In my times of *perplexity*, when I have not found direction, He is my *pilot* and will get me back on the right course. He is *perfect*, fully informed, complete and skilled. He is *patient* and quick to understand. He is the *peace-speaker*—the One Who speaks *peace* into my heart. He is the *potter* and I am the clay. He is my *provider* and my *protector*. He is my *promise*, the man of great expectations. In His *presence*, there if fullness of joy.

He is my *promoter*, encouraging me to advance. He is *pure*—He has no ulterior motives for me, only wholesome and unselfish motives. When I realized this, I wrote a jingle that goes like this: *I'm pressing on, I'm pressing on, I'm not regressing, I'm redressing with my righteous gear, so I'll have no fear, may shed some tears, but I'm pressing on.* He is deserving of all my *praise*.

Scriptures

Galatians 4:5	Matthew 19:26
Psalm 23:3	Psalm 84:11
Philippians 3:12-13	1 Corinthians 3:9
Romans 2:4	Philippians 4:7
Philippians 4:7	Mark 4:39
Hebrews 5:9	Isaiah 64:8
Matthew 13:46	Psalm 16:11
Ephesians 4:8-9	Psalm 75:6
Luke 12:32	Isaiah 42:8

If you know it, sing this song now and several times throughout your day to remind you of who you are *in Christ,* who He is and what He can do *in you*, and what you can do *in Him.*

Peace, Peace, Wonderful Peace

Peace, peace wonderful peace,
Coming down from the father above,
Sweep over my spirit forever I pray,
In fathomless billows of love.

By: Warren D. Comel and W. George Cooper

Peace Speaker

I know the Peace Speaker,
I know him by Name,
I know the Peace Speaker,
He can calm the wind and waves,
When He says, "Peace be still," they have to obey.
I'm glad I know the Peace Speaker,
Yes, I know Him by name.

By : Geron Davis/BMI

Answer these questions: 1. Which statement stands out to me the most? 2. How could my life be different if I truly believed it were true? 3. What am I willing to change today to move forward?

_____

_____

_____

_____

_____

_____

_____

Psalm 48:1

Great is the Lord, and greatly to be praised
In the city of our God, In His holy mountain.

PROMISE OF POWER

"Behold, I send the Promise of My Father upon you; but tarry in the city of Jerusalem until you are endued with power from on high"
(Luke 24:49).

Q

Jesus is my *qualifier*. He has enabled the Holy Spirit to *quicken* my mortal body. He has *quenched* my thirst. He has *quieted* my soul. His Word is *quick*, powerful and sharper than any two-edged sword. He is *quick*—brisk, swift, keen, and sensitive.

Because Jesus is my *qualifier*, He is the One who gives me proper and suitable *qualities*. I am *qualified* and fit. I have a degree of excellence only He can impart.

If that same Spirit that raised Him from the dead dwells in me, it will q*uicken* my mortal body and raise me from the dead and all of my, unproductive works. This means the Holy Spirit will stimulate me, resuscitate me and will make me come alive in Him.

My thirst is always *quenched* when I drink of living water. His well never runs dry and all I need to do is drink.

Scriptures

2 Corinthians 3:5-6	Psalm 25:20
Romans 8:11	Hebrews 4:12
John 4:14	

If you know it, sing this song now and several times throughout your day to remind you of who you are *in Christ,* who He is and what He can do *in you*, and what you can do *in Him*.

Qualified Overcomer

I'm a qualified overcomer,
I'm a qualified overcomer,
I'm a qualified overcomer
Through the blood of the lamb,
I'm a qualified overcomer,
Qualified overcomer,
Qualified overcomer through the blood.

By: Lari Goss

Answer these questions: 1. Which statement stands out to me the most? 2. How could my life be different if I truly believed it were true? 3. What am I willing to change today to move forward?

_____

_____

_____

_____

_____

_____

_____

Hebrews 4:12

For the word of God is quick, and powerful, and sharper than any twoedged sword... (King James Version).

QUIETNESS

*"In returning and rest
you shall be saved;
in quietness and confidence
shall be your strength*
(Isaiah 30:15).

R

Jesus is the *restorer* of the breach. He is the One who *re-establishes relationship* between God and man. He *refurbishes, reconditions, reinstates.* He *renews* and completely overhauls. He is the *resurrection* and the life. He *revitalizes.* He is the *redeemer.* He will *reign* forever. He will *rebuke, reprimand* and scold the devourer for my sake. The *righteous* shall flourish like a palm tree and shall grow like a cedar in Lebanon. They will bear fruit even in their senior years!

Jesus *restored* my soul. He is my *Redeemer,* the *rock* of ages, my *rock* in this weary land. He is my *rest.* He *revives* me. I can *rejoice* in Him. He has *received* me. He has *reconciled* me. He is my *refuge.* I can *rely* on Him. I can *rejoice* in Him. He is one who *reward*s those who diligently seek Him. He *refines* me as pure gold. He is my *Rose* of Sharon. I will *run* my *race* with patience. I have never seen the *righteous*—those who are in *right-standing* with Him—forsaken, nor His seed begging for bread.

Scriptures

Isaiah 58:12
Ephesians 2:14
2 Corinthians 5:17
John 11:25
Isaiah 63:16
Hebrews 1:8
Malachi 3:11

Psalm 92:12
Psalm 23:3
Hebrews 11:6
Song of Solomon 2:1
Hebrews 12:1
Psalm 37:25

If you know it, sing this song now and several times throughout your day to remind you of who you are *in Christ,* who He is and what He can do *in you,* and what you can do *in Him.*

There's Room at the Cross for You

There's room at the cross for you,
There's room at the cross for you.
Though millions have come,
There is still room for one.
Yes, there's room at the cross for you.

The hand of my savior is strong,
And the love of my savior is long;
Through sunshine or rain
Through loss or in gain,
The blood flows from Calvary
To cleanse every stain.

By: Ira F. Stanphill (1946)

Answer these questions: 1. Which statement stands out to me the most? 2. How could my life be different if I truly believed it were true? 3. What am I willing to change today to move forward?

_____

_____

_____

_____

_____

_____

_____

John 11:25

"I am the resurrection and the life,
He who believes in Me, though he may die, he shall live."

REDEEMER

Christ has redeemed us
from the curse of the law,
having become a curse for us
for it is written,
"Cursed is everyone who hangs on a tree"
(Galatians 3:13).

S

Jesus is the *Savior*, the *seed* of David, and the *Good Shepherd*. He is the only *sure* foundation on which to build. He is the *Son* of the highest. He is *salvation*. Jesus made the ultimate *sacrifice*. He is the *seed* of Abraham and the *Sun of Righteousness*.

He *satisfies* my mouth with good things. He *sealed* me. He *saved* me. I am *safe* in Him. He *satisfies* my longing soul. As my *Savior*, He made the ultimate *sacrifice* just for me; therefore, I know that He will withhold no good thing from me! I am *saved*, delivered, made whole and complete in Him. He walks with me through every *season* of my life. When winter has been longer than planned, He brings me the *Spring-time* that I need. I can dwell in the *secret* place of the Most High and abide under the *shadow* of the Almighty. *surely* He will deliver me from the *snare* of the fowler. Jesus will *set* me free from anything that tries to catch me or entrap me.

I will *seek* Jesus today while He may be found. He *seeks* me and *saves* me when I am lost. He left the *splendor* of heaven to be my *substitute* on earth.

Because He is my cornerstone, a *sure* foundation for me, and I trust in Him, I never have to be ashamed or flee in *sudden* panic because of dreadful circumstances (see Isaiah 28:16, in the *Amplified Bible*).

74

Scriptures

John 1:29
John 7:41-43
John 10:11, 14
Isaiah 28:16 (*Amplified Bible*)
Mark 5:7
Acts 4:12
Philippians 2:8
Galatians 3:29
Malachi 4:2

Psalm 103:5
2 Timothy 2:19
Psalm 107:9
Psalm 91:1, 3
John 8:32
Isaiah 55:6
Matthew 18:12
Philippians 2:8

If you know it, sing this song now and several times throughout your day to remind you of who you are *in Christ,* who He is and what He can do *in you,* and what you can do *in Him.*

Surely the Presence of the Lord Is in This Place

Surely the presence of the Lord is in this place,
I can feel His mighty power and His grace,
I can feel the brush of angels' wings,
I see glory on each face,
Surely the presence of the Lord is in this place.

By: : Lanny Wolf

Answer these questions: 1. Which statement stands out to me the most? 2. How could my life be different if I truly believed it were true? 3. What am I willing to change today to move forward?

_____

_____

_____

_____

_____

_____

_____

Titus 2:11

*For the grace of God that brings salvation
has appeared to all men.*

SEEK HIM

Seek the Lord while He may be found,
Call upon Him while He is near
(Isaiah 55:6).

T

Jesus is the *truth*, the life and the way. He is certain in all of His ways. He is accurate and legitimate. He says that He knows the *thoughts* that He thinks toward us, *thoughts* of peace and not of evil, to bring us to an expected end. His *thoughts* are not our thoughts. He does not go by our *time* clock. He is an on-time God. He is a strong *tower*, the righteous can run into it and be saved. There is no shadow of *turning* in Him.

He is my *teacher* and my *tutor*. He is the *truth*. He has made me to *triumph* over the devil. As my strong tower, I can run into Him, *trust* in Him, and be safe. He is my friend in whom I can *trust* and follow. He will not mislead me, distract me, or discourage me. His devotion and loyalty are sincere toward me because I know that He will never *turn* away from me.

Scriptures

John 14:6   James 1:17
Jeremiah 29:11   John 14:26
Isaiah 55:11   1 John 3:8
Proverbs 18:10

If you know it, sing this song now and several times throughout your day to remind you of who you are *in Christ,* who He is and what He can do *in you*, and what you can do *in Him*.

'Tis So Sweet to Trust in Jesus

'Tis so sweet to trust in Jesus,
Just to take Him at His word;
Just to rest upon his promise,
Just to know, thus saith the Lord.

Jesus, Jesus, how I trust Him!
How I've proved him o'er and o'er!
Jesus, Jesus, precious Jesus!
O for grace to trust Him more.

By: Louisa M. R. Stead

Answer these questions: 1. Which statement stands out to me the most? 2. How could my life be different if I truly believed it were true? 3. What am I willing to change today to move forward?

_____

_____

_____

_____

_____

_____

_____

John 14:6-7

"I am the way, the truth, and the life. No one comes to the Father except through Me. If you had known Me, you would have known My Father also; and from now on you know Him and have seen Him."

80

TRUTH IS LIBERATING

*"If you abide in My word,
you are My disciples indeed.
And you shall know the truth,
and the truth shall make you free
(John 8:31b-32).*

U

Jesus is God's *unspeakable* gift. He is *upright* and respectable. He brings *unity*. He *upholds* all things with the word of His power. His *unconditional* love is *unlimited* and absolute. He is *unique*—there is no one else like Him. His love and thoughts toward me are *unrestricted* and *unrestrained*.

I like to think of it this way. There are two beings on earth with *unconditional* love. They have the same letters in their names and the same number of letters! G-O-D and D-O-G. You may not agree with me, but I am grateful that God loves me enough to give me a dog who demonstrates *unconditional* love. They are both devoted to me, forgiving, loyal, and trustworthy. They both like me, want to be with me, and neither one will ever leave me or forsake me. There is nothing like the supernatural love of God; its resources are *unlimited*.

Scriptures

2 Corinthians 9:15	1 Chronicles 17:20
Psalm 25:8	Psalm 139:17-19
Hebrews 1:3	

If you know it, sing this song now and several times throughout your day to remind you of who you are *in Christ*, who He is and what He can do *in you*, and what you can do *in Him*.

Joy Unspeakable

It is joy unspeakable and full of glory,
Full of glory, full of glory.
It is joy unspeakable and full of glory
And the half has never yet been told.
By: Barney E. Warren (1900)

Answer these questions: 1. Which statement stands out to me the most? 2. How could my life be different if I truly believed it were true? 3. What am I willing to change today to move forward?

_____

_____

_____

_____

_____

_____

_____

Proverbs 3:13

Happy is the man who finds wisdom, And the man who gains understanding;
For her proceeds are better than the profits of silver,
And her gain than fine gold.

V

Jesus is the *vine* and the *vinedresser*. He is *valliant*. He is the *victorious* one. His presence is no longer *veiled* or obscure. He can be known intimately. He is the pearl of great price, to be *valued* above all other treasure. He generously shares this treasure through earthen *vessels*. He is the One who owns the right to take *vengeance*, who is just and fair. His *voice* is as the sound of many waters.

I am a branch on His *vine*. His life flows in and through me and produces fruit. He carefully watches over me as a worker in the *vine* to protect the life, the growth, and the fruit. He has made me a *vessel* of honor, a receptacle carrying His message and His life. This is a high and noble purpose. I will be *vigilant* and stay alert and protect the message and life that He has instilled in me. I will remain *virtuous*, moral and upright. I will remain *victorious*. I will keep my *vows* that I made to Him when I committed my life to Him. I pledge with my honor. I will lift my *voice* and sing praises to Him as long as I live. I honor this *valuable*, precious treasure in my life. I have no need to be *vengeful*, because I hear His *voice* as the sound of many waters saying, "*Vengeance* is mine...I will repay." Knowing He is fair and just, I can pray for those who despitefully use me, and bless those who curse me because He will take on my cause and defend me. He thinks this is the right thing to do!

Scriptures

John 15:4-6	2 Timothy 2:20
Revelation 3:21	1 Peter 5:8
2 Corinthians 3:12-14	2 Peter 1:2-6
Philippians 3:10	Psalm 116:14, 18
2 Corinthians 4:7	Psalm 104:33
Romans 12:19	Matthew 5:44

Scriptures (Continued)

Revelation 1:15   Luke 18:1-8

If you know it, sing this song now and several times throughout your day to remind you of who you are *in Christ,* who He is and what He can do *in you*, and what you can do *in Him*.

Victory in Jesus

I heard an old, old story,
How a Savior came from glory.
How He gave His life on Calvary,
To save a wretch like me;
I heard about His groaning,
Of His precious blood atoning,
Then I repented of my sin
And won the Victory.

Oh, victory in Jesus, my Savior forever,
He sought me and He bought me
With His redeeming blood.
He loved me ere I knew Him
And all my love is due Him.
He plunged me to Victory
Beneath the cleansing flood.

By: Burl Ives

Answer these questions: 1. Which statement stands out to me the most? 2. How could my life be different if I truly believed it were true? 3. What am I willing to change today to move forward?

_____

_____

_____

_____

_____

_____

_____

1 Corinthians 15:57

But thanks be to God, who gives us the victory
Through our Lord Jesus Christ.

FAITH THAT BRINGS
THE VICTORY

For whatever is born of God
overcomes the world.
And this is
the victory that has
overcome the world—our faith
(1 John 5:4).

W

Jesus is the *way*, the truth, and the life. He is *Wonderful*, Counselor, the Mighty God and Prince of Peace. He is the *word* of God made flesh. He upholds all things with the *word* of his power. He is living *water* for the thirsty. He *washes* away all sin. He is the One who *watches* over us. He is a *way-maker*, one who makes a way when there seems to be no way to go. He is *wise*.

"Need I *wander* if God loves me, need I *wonder* if He cares? To realize that in every phase of my life, He's there to guide. He inspires me in such confidence, it makes me want to sing. Need I *wonder*, Yes, I know that God cares" (Song by Fred Conscio).

Let this song inspire you and encourage you to find your true identity in Christ. I have discovered through personal experience, not mere mental assent, that God loves me. The restlessness and inner turmoil stopped. The love of Jesus ended the nomadic impulses, gave me rest and I gained repose in Him. Since Jesus has *washed* my sins away, now I know that He can take care of all other issues in my life. I have turned over everything to Him and have given Him full responsibility of my life. He is *wise* in all of His *ways*. He is my *way-maker*, and I trust Him to make a *way* for me when it looks as if I am at a dead-end road and there is no *way* out. He is *worthy* of all my praise.

Scriptures

John 14:5-7   John 4:9-11
Isaiah 9:6   1 Corinthians 10:13
John 1:14, 17   1 John 1:9
Hebrews 1:3   1 Timothy 1:17

If you know it, sing this song now and several times throughout your day to remind you of who you are *in Christ,* who He is and what He can do *in you,* and what you can do *in Him.*

What a Friend

What a friend we have in Jesus,
All our sins and grief to bear.
What a privilege to carry
Everything to God in prayer.

When we walk with the Lord,
In the light of His Word,
What a glory He sheds on our way!
Let us do His good will,
He abides with us still,
And with all who will trust and obey.
Trust and obey, for there's no other way
To be happy in Jesus, but to trust and obey.

> By: Charles C. Converse (1834-1918) and Joseph M. Scriven who wrote it for his mother across the seas in Ireland)

Answer these questions: 1. Which statement stands out to me the most? 2. How could my life be different if I truly believed it were true? 3. What am I willing to change today to move forward?

_____

_____

_____

_____

_____

_____

_____

Ephesians 4:1

I, therefore, the prisoner of the Lord,
beseech you to have a walk worthy of the calling
with which you were called.

WAIT ON GOD

Wait on the Lord;
Be of good courage,
And He shall strengthen your heart;
Wait, I say on the Lord!
(Psalm 27:14).

X-Y-Z

Just as a copy machine multiplies copies of an original document, Jesus *Xeroxed* Himself by way of living in human beings. He made us a mirror image of Himself. By becoming flesh, He multiplied His influence to the world by commissioning and commanding us to share His message with all others. He suffered the death of a cross so that by the grace of God He might taste death for everyone.

He is *Yahweh*. He is a Yoke-bearer. He *yearns* to be kind and loving toward and to show mercy. All of His promises are "*Yea* and Amen."

Scriptures

John 1:14   Isaiah 30:18
Hebrews 1:9   2 Corinthians 1:20
Matthew 11:28-30

If you know them, sing these songs now and several times throughout your day to remind you of who you are *in Christ,* who He is and what He can do *in you*, and what you can do *in Him*.

Yes, Lord

I'm trading my sorrow.
I'm trading my shame
I'm laying them down, for the joy of the Lord.
Yes, Lord, Yes Lord, yes, yes, Lord
Yes, Lord, yes Lord, yes, yes Lord...

By: Israel and New Breed

Zion

Zion is calling me to a higher place of praise
To stand upon the mountain to magnify His name
To tell all the people and every nation He reigns
Zion is calling me to a higher place of praise.

By: Clint Brown

Answer these questions: 1. Which statement stands out to me the most? 2. How could my life be different if I truly believed it were true? 3. What am I willing to change today to move forward?

_____

_____

_____

_____

_____

_____

_____

_____

Titus 2:14

Who (Jesus Christ) gave Himself for us, that He might redeem us from every lawless deed and purify for Himself His own special people, zealous for good works..

In Loving Memory of Billie June McKee—
My "Mama Billie"

Mama Billie was my intercessor, my friend, and one of my greatest fans and supporters. She loved to hear me sing.

I met Mama Billie in 1968 while traveling with Nancy Harmon and the Victory Voices. At that time Mama Billie and her sweet hubby Charles said they would have adopted me had they known I was adoptable in spite of my age. Then, when Billie Jane "BJ" Watkins and her husband David, with much love, adopted me in 1976, and it was ironic, because instead of being unwanted, it was the first time I was up for grabs!

Mama Billie stayed close to me through all the years. I was with her when her hubby passed away, and then again when she went home to be with the Lord. I was honored to speak at both of their celebration services. God has been so good to me.

Thank you, Mama Billie, for the years and the unconditional love you invested in me.

We get stuck in life because we don't know who we are, where we are going or how to get there. We lack confidence, security and competency because we feel powerless. We find the power to become unstuck when we realize who we are *in Christ.* This innate power thrusts us out of the muck and mire which are holding us back. It brings us the greatest joy and peace and it pleases God when we experience it.

The purpose of this devotional is to remind you of your identity in Christ and His identity in you. It can help you overcome the lies you believe which have kept you stuck in the past, such as *God could never use me, I'm not good enough to succeed,* or *I'm not worthy to succeed.* God believes you are good enough and that you are worthy enough. When your inherent beliefs match the truth of God's Word, you will find the power to change. The reminders in this devotional are signposts showing the way. Allow them to guide you in your journey onward and upward.

Ellen Zakaria Roachelle has been in ministry for over 44 years. After studying cosmetology, she received ministry training from Bethany Bible College, Nancy Harmon Ministries, The Therapon Institute™, and in her words, "The School of Hard Knocks." Her experience, in addition to traveling with Nancy Harmon includes working with women with substance abuse problems at The Hope Center, in Sweet Home, Oregon, and pioneering The Ministry Center Church, in Lebanon, Oregon, as well as serving as its pastor.

Ellen and Jim Roachelle

$12.99
ISBN 978-0-615-66177-3
51299>

9 780615 661773

www.ingramcontent.com/pod-product-compliance
Lightning Source LLC
Chambersburg PA
CBHW070525030426
42337CB00016B/2116